Life Coach

Discover Your Purpose

Do What You Love and Live a Purpose Driven Life

Dan Miller

Legal Disclaimer

Table of Content

1: What is Purpose?
2: Keys to Discovering Your Passion
3: Setting Goals that Fuel Your Purpose
4: Being Proactive
5: Starting Out with the End in Mind
6: Leveraging on Positive Visualizations
7: Mastering the Science of Personal Management
8: Overcoming Negativity and Fostering Resilience
9: Leveraging on Coaching and Mentorship for Personal Development
10: Living a Balanced Life
Conclusion

Important Insight

There is a written rule that some people will succeed no matter how little they try and that others will fail irrespective of how hard they try. The truth is we all live in an existential framework where we are presented with opportunities to pursue our purpose. Despite the odds that are stacked against a considerable portion of humanity, few people have successfully attained their goals.

One interesting thing is that these people do not necessarily come from privileged backgrounds but they have one thing in common; they were able to seize the opportunities available, work hard and ultimately they became prosperous. They live purpose driven lives. When you look at the available data on the lives of successful people, you will find that because of their determination, they have formed a solid support system and have a well researched and sophisticated toolkit that they use to confront challenges.

Determined people are not successful by default but rather they have trained themselves to always think and troubleshoot before undertaking projects and pursuing a certain cause. In their toolkit contain valuable information, amongst them resourceful people and mentors, ways to cope with uncertainty and negativity, positive visualizations, goal setting techniques and alternative course of actions.

With this determination, you cannot afford to scroll through life without a clear understanding of your inner potential, goals and personal strengths. To understand your purpose, you have to set aside a quiet time to deeply think about the things that make you truly happy. This is your path of passion and the moment you discover it, pursue it to the very end.

1: What is Purpose?

One of the driving forces that have spurred research into social behavior and personal development is purpose. As people become gradually aware of whom they are, they feel the need to discover more about their life's purpose and existence. The best approach to adopt when discussing and delving into the concept of purpose is having the knowledge of what purpose is and how different it is from goals and religiosity.

Purpose refers to a cognitive process that defines your goals in life and provides you with a personal meaning. It is a central self-organizing aim that stimulates goals, manages behavior and gives you the essence of existence. By guiding the use of finite personal resources, purpose directs your decisions and goals in life. Instead of governing your behavior, purpose just offers direction similar to a compass offering direction to a navigator. Following your purpose is purely optional but there are benefits of doing so.

Living in accordance to your purpose makes you a self-sustaining force and an aggressive agent in goal pursuit and goal attainment. Purpose is therefore crucial in helping us to organize our lives and develop persistence that resonates across time and context.

The Difference between Purpose and Goals

Although they are constantly mentioned together in research and conversational context, purpose and goals are not synonymous. Goals are more precise in their impact on proximal behaviors. They focus on a specific end point and serve to guide our behavior either towards or away from the end point. Purpose on the other hand is a broader component that influences behavior and stimulates goals. Purpose does not point you towards a designated outcome but rather it motivates you to be goal oriented. Unlike goals which have terminal outcomes, purpose and values just give you the general direction of life.

Another way to look at purpose is to view it as a goal manager. People who have a purpose in their lives move seamlessly from goal to goal or have the capacity to manage multiple goals simultaneously. On the other hand, people without a purpose may succeed in achieving one goal, but immediately afterwards they find it extremely difficult to identify another goal. Goals therefore act as the center point and are produced and inspired by purpose.

The Dimensions of Purpose

Purpose lies on a three dimensional continuum consisting of strength, scope and awareness. Scope refers to the extent to which your purpose affects your life. For instance, a purpose that influences all your thoughts, actions and emotions is said to have a broad scope. A purpose of a narrow scope is more organized, but it does not influence a greater range of behaviors compared to a purpose of a broad scope.

Strength is the tendency for the purpose to influence your thoughts, actions and emotions on the domains relevant to its scope. A strong purpose powerfully influences behaviors relevant to your purpose. Combined with scope, strength dictates the extent to which purpose affects your health, longevity and well-being. For example, a purpose that is characterized by great strength and a broader scope has a more pronounced effect. In addition, a strong and broad purpose brings resilience to obstacles and barriers to progress.

Awareness reflects the extent to which a person is knowledgeable and can articulate his purpose. It is strongly affected by scope and strength. Consider for a moment the analogy of gravity. On earth, the force of gravity is broader in scope but weak in its impact. As we live our lives, we don't pay particular attention to gravitational forces. However, if we were to be taken to another planet such as Jupiter which has twice as much gravitational force as earth, our awareness of the force of gravity would substantially increase.

Behaviors consistent with purpose can be activated to provide motivation for action. When a person is aware of a purpose, it will require him less effort to pursue than one who is totally unaware.

Pursuit of Multiple Purposes

It is not unusual for a person to have multiple life purposes. However, multiple purposes can be beneficial only to a certain point after which such purposes serve to reduce the resource allocation.

For instance, if you pursue a single purpose, you may become discouraged if the obstacles you face become too great to surmount. On the other hand, if you have several purposes which are independent from each other, then the moment you encounter an obstacle in one you automatically shift your attention and focus to the other purposes. This shifting between life purposes enhances your pursuit for purposeful living and may increase the chances of positive results.

Multiple purposes, however, may result into constant switching from one purpose to the other and this can hinder progress. For a well balanced and sustainable approach, you need a manageable number of life purposes to which you can allocate adequate resources and focus on so as to reap tangible benefits.

Critical Elements of Purpose

For you to live a purposeful life; there are elements that are essential. These elements are:

Consistent Behavior

This serves as the motivating force to help you overcome obstacles, maintain focus on your goals and seek alternative means irrespective of the changing environmental conditions. Purposeful people are more consistent in their behaviors in both their private and public lives.

Psychological Flexibility

In light of changing demands, opportunities and obstacles, purpose enables you to be more flexible. Avoiding hardships by flexibly managing your environmental both the psychological and physical will enable you to experience fewer problems compared to those who live without a purpose.

Efficient Resource Allocation

Purpose makes it possible for you to efficiently allocate the available personal resources including time and energy into pursuing the purpose. Any other wasteful actions and behaviors are kept at bay and the resources they would have consumed are re-injected back to the purpose oriented actions.

These elements can also be interpreted as the necessary ingredients to a purposeful life. Without them, it becomes impossible to discover and achieve your purpose in life.

2: Keys to Discovering Your Passion

Most people try to justify their failure and uncertainties in life to not having enough passion in one thing or another. This causes them to be in a continuous cycle of boring and uninteresting things. Contrary to the belief of many people, discovering what you love is not as difficult as it seems. Passion is not a precious commodity that is reserved for a select few. Rather, it is a gift that every one of us has been endowed with. The only thing we need to do to exploit our passion is to have the right attitude. Work is supposed to be fun, and therefore, you must take time to explore what makes you tick.

Instead of seeing yourself as hopeless because you have not discovered your passion, start visualizing yourself as being surrounded by endless possibilities. The reality is that your imagination is the only limit you have to be doing what you love. In order to breakthrough from this cocoon of uncertainty and lack of passion, there are simple and straightforward keys that will lead you into finding your purpose and meaning in life.

Give Yourself an Opportunity to be Passionate

This is often considered an ordinary and immaterial step in discovering your passion despite its great significance. The reason why you are not pursuing what you love doing could be that you think you do not deserve to be passionate about what you do. On the contrary, everyone has the right to be passionate with what they do for a living or otherwise. You need to wake up excited about your life because you have every right to do so. When you give yourself permission to passionately pursue what you do, you will be in a much better position to help others as well.

In order to resonate, accept and love what you do. You need to modify your mental picture. The moment you align your identity with your passion then it becomes much easier for you to find fulfillment in the things you do.

Allow Yourself to Venture and Explore

There exists one true passion for each one of us, and everything else is not worth our efforts and focus. This creates the all or nothing mindset. The danger with this perspective is that it makes you miss out on other opportunities in your disposal for living passionately.

There is a spectrum of possibilities between your fulfillment and enjoyment of what you do. At one end of the spectrum lies the work that you despise and cannot do under all circumstances. The other end of the spectrum is the work that you love and the mere thought of it brings excitement and energy. Between these two points lies a huge range of possibilities for work that bores, work that makes you feel indifferent, work that challenges and stimulates you as well as tasks that make you come alive with excitement.

Your best move should be towards the direction of what makes you come alive. As you pursue what you love, you will come across options that will lead you to the ultimate purpose of your life. The more aggressive and passionately you move towards the work that excites you, the more efficient you will become at filtering out every other thing that drains you and distracts you from your desired end.

One important thing to note is that you will first have to grow accustomed to liking your work before you actually love it. Do not spend too much time with an attitude that dreads work because this will blind you, deplete you and turn you away from your passion.

Take a Closer Look at What You are Currently Doing

The opportunities for doing what we love lie right under our noses. We have a tendency to think that we cannot make a meaningful living out of what we do. By changing our perspectives, we may find that the things we have been looking down upon actually are the most fascinating and exciting.

Take Time and Question Yourself

Most people have never asked themselves powerful questions in an attempt to figure out what they are passionate about. You need to give yourself time and let go of other activities so that you can engage yourself intensively with your passion.

We often let other things take precedence at the expense of exploring the things that excite us. For you to succeed in finding your passion, you need to set apart quality time and just figure out what makes you excited. Some of the powerful questions that can lead you to your passion and your purpose are:

- What would you do even if you did not get paid for it?
- Do you have any special gifts that you can share with the world?
- When specific time in your life did you felt most creative?
- What comes naturally for you?
- What have you accomplished in the past that was successful?

These questions will awaken your subconscious mind and you will begin searching within yourself to find your passion. In answering the above questions, do not think too much. Just allow yourself to jot down anything that comes to your mind. Instead of censoring yourself, allow the link to form between your fingertips and your heart. You can always remove things that do not make sense later. Looking at your answers, there should be a pattern that is showing.

You May Have to Create Your Passion

Not everything that you are passionate about exists. There are some things that do not exist as of yet, but you are all the same passionate about them. For instance, computer programmers could be passionate about software that doesn't exist yet, but through this passion they slowly visualize and ultimately bring it into existence. At times, you may have to create your profession by bridging the gaps between different fields. You should not limit yourself to the template-like and conventional paths. There are always deficiencies you can fill in and create a purpose out of that.

Always Test Your Passion

Before you incur expenses or take yourself down a certain path, you should test your passion to establish its credibility. You can do this by taking simple self-help courses online or at your local colleges to figure out if you have real passion in the area that you want to specialize in. You can also buy a number of books just to establish how long you can sustain your interest reading them. Alternatively, you can also find someone who is doing what you are aspiring to do and may send them an email or get in touch with them for a simple interview. Going through the testing process will inform you whether the passion is real or just a fleeting fantasy with no possibility for a long term fulfillment.

Look for Fulfillment instead of Happiness

There is a clear difference between fulfillment and happiness. People spend hundreds or thousands of hours trying to find a career that will bring true happiness to their lives. The problem with this approach is that happiness is not a defined concept, but rather a vague one. You may enjoy riding a horse or eating ice cream, but that may not necessarily be your passion. Most of the things that make you happy are just for temporarily enjoyment. The reality is that you can be truly happy without being fulfilled.

Some of the work that gives you fulfillment may not necessarily make you a celebrity or an extremely rich person. However, this kind of work aligns with your values. If you value community, relationships, and making a positive impact in whatever you do, this is most likely your passion.

After you have found your passion, start living it right away. It pays to immerse yourself in a passionate and deliberate action rather than toe-dipping perpetually.

3: Setting Goals that Fuel Your Purpose

Goal setting is an important foundation for success. It is because goals help us concentrate our energy and actions on the end result while at the same time it measures our progress with respect to the goals that we set. In practice however, many would acknowledge the existence of a gap between goal setting familiarity and the true mastery of the ability to develop and communicate powerful goals that produce sustained action and at the same time generate transformational results.

There are clear links between motivation, performance and goal setting. Other than imposing goals on yourself, you should use goal setting as a tool to create a sense of direction and purpose. The goal setting environment is critical because it provides the conditions necessary for you to be effective in whatever you do.

The Importance of Goals in Purposeful Living

According to Locke and Latham (2002), a goal refers to the object or aim of an action. It reflects your purpose and points you towards the expected quality, quantity or rate of performance. As a process, goal setting always creates discrepancies because of the gap between our current situation and the desired future state. In addition, the process of goal setting affects our overall level of motivation, our belief system and our capabilities to perform.

The discrepancy that is created by goal setting is to be interpreted as a constructive discontent that motivates us towards persistent and sustainable goal-relevant behavior. There are three conditions which are to be met if the goal setting process is to be motivating. These conditions are:

You should feel that you have a capacity to achieve the goals. This capacity can be derived from your current stock of resources and from the additional expertise or support you require in due course.

Commitment from your part

You should be ready to have "whatever it takes" attitude to achieve your goals. Lack of commitment leads to lack of motivation.

Specific and unambiguous goals

Specific goals make it easy to access progress and adjust your pace accordingly.

Goal-Directed Behavior and Happiness

Goal-oriented action is one of the key elements of goal setting theory. Without a goal-directed action, it is impossible for you to achieve your purpose, let alone being happy. Most of us remember a time where we were so engrossed in an activity that we became totally disengaged from everything else around us. According to research, this is a moment when our emotional state is most active.

Negative emotions such as fear, sadness, anxiety or boredom produce what is known as psychic entropy. This is a state in which we cannot focus our attention on anything else because we need that very attention to restore our inner order. Positive emotions, on the other hand, including happiness, alertness or excitement are known as psychic negentropy. At this state, we don't require attention to ruminate and feel sorry for ourselves, thus we can direct that attention fully into whatever task we are executing.

Goals are usually arranged in order of hierarchy from the trivial ones to the more important ones. In the course of an ordinary day, about a third of the people do what they do because they have nothing better to do. Another third do the things they do because they have to do them. The last third do the things they do out of love. These proportions can change with respect to gender, age and the kind of activities.

The most interesting thing is that people feel best when they do something voluntarily and feel worse when they are engaged in something as an obligation. Psychic entropy is at its highest when people do something because they have nothing else to do. Goal setting is therefore important as a means to give focus and bring motivation into the task that is lying ahead.

Harnessing the Power of Goal Setting

There are a powerful set of tools we can use to put goal setting to work. These tools take human dynamics into account as they help us in generating goals that lead to purposeful and effective behavior.

Self Efficacy

The concept of efficacy is very important to setting and achieving personal goals. Efficacy is the belief that you hold about your ability to perform a certain task. These beliefs affect the manner in which we set goals and the choices that we make about the activities we are about to engage in. Efficacy can also refer to the measure of how much effort you are willing to expend and the length of time you will persist in the face of difficulty or failure.

Specific goals lead to higher performance as compared to urging people to do their best.

Setting short-term sub-goals raises self efficacy when compared to a situation where only long-term goals exist. Goals should be challenging, clear and consisting of a target and a timeframe.

Provision of support can help in increasing mastery that ultimately leads to successful outcomes. The support can be in the form of role modeling or mentorship.

The level of self-confidence should be commensurate with the level of goal difficulty.

Task Complexity

When setting goals for complex tasks, ensure that you include short-term goals because they give immediate guidelines and incentives for better performance. Long-term goals alone can be too far removed and difficult to connect with.

Setting goals requires subject-specific knowledge, realistic expectations and appropriate strategies on how to get a task done.

Goal Commitment

When you are committed to your goals, the relationship between the goals and your performance becomes stronger. As the goals become more difficult, the level of commitment has to be raised to inject the effort required to attain the goals. The two main categories of factors that are required in enhancing goal commitment are self-belief and prioritization. You have to belief that you can indeed attain the goals set as well as making goal attainment a priority over everything else. The rationale or purpose of the goals set must be clear in order for them to motivate us. To succeed in attaining goals, you have to link them to the bigger picture.

Feedback

For goal setting to be effective, it has to be combined with the appropriate feedback. Timely feedback provides the necessary information about whether your picture of reality is aligned with what is required to achieve the goals. Providing ongoing feedback indicates that you are paying attention to your progress towards your set goals.

Satisfaction

Satisfaction tends to increase when you exceed your goals. As the number of successes increase, your total satisfaction also grows. To incorporate satisfaction in goal setting, you should set challenging goals that increase your interest. It will help you discover the pleasurable aspects in getting the task done.

The Common Pitfalls in Goal Setting

There are a number of pitfalls that you may encounter when setting your goals. Knowing how to maneuver around each of these pitfalls will give you the advantage of setting goals that bring satisfaction and a sense of achievement.

Goal Content Pitfalls

Setting goals that are too difficult or idealized can lead to failure. Difficult goals lead to poor performance because they stretch you beyond your zone of knowledge and skills. Idealized goals on the other hand can lead to inappropriate actions that are aimed at attaining the goal irrespective of the cost and consequences.

To avoid this pitfall, you need to develop your capacity and enhance your knowledge and skills necessary for goal attainment. You should also examine the potential risks in every goal and be flexible enough to abandon it if the results are not forthcoming within a reasonable time.

Goal Setting Process Pitfalls

Setting conflicting goals can limit your potential and bring disorder in goal attainment. Ensure that all goals are aligned towards your purpose which is the bigger picture. Conflicting goals rob each other of resources and the attainment of one undermines the other. When setting goals, ensure that your words and actions are streamlined to avoid possible instances of conflict.

The Impact Pitfall

At times, the goals you set may bring a negative perception where you perceive them more as threats rather than challenges. Also, tying rewards to success in goal attainment can lead to overstatement of performance, particularly in cases where you are closer to attaining your goals. This is unethical and it can lead to destructive self behavior. Where the number of goals is large, they may cause stress and underachievement. To eliminate this pitfall, you should be true to yourself in goal setting and pick a manageable number of goals depending on your capacity.

When done well, goal setting can act as the fuel to drive you towards your purpose.

4: Being Proactive

As a person, you are directly responsible for your own life. Your behavior is a sum of all your decisions and not your conditions. You are the only one with the initiative and the responsibility to turn things around and make them happen. Proactive people are conscious of their purpose and they know that the conditions and circumstances around them are not to blame but rather their own behavior.

Your behavior is a product of your conscious choice based on your value systems. By nature, we are proactive beings and in the event our lives are conditioned by the events around us, it is because we have consciously made a decision to empower those things to control us.

The opposite of pro-activeness is re-activeness. People who are reactive are affected by the physical environment more than their own value system. If the weather around them is good then everything else is fine their attitude and performance is not affected.

Proactive people are masters of their destiny and purpose and they carry their own weather with them. Whether it rains or not, it makes absolutely no difference to them. Since they are driven by value, they will produce quality work.

Reactive people are affected by the social environment meaning that when people treat them well they feel good and when they don't, they become protective or defensive. They build their emotional lives around the habits and behaviors of others. To some extent, reactive people empower the weaknesses of other people to take control of them.

For you to live a purposeful life, you need to subordinate an impulse to a value that is central to your existence. Even though from time to time you may be influenced by external stimuli, your response to the stimuli should be value based. In the words of Eleanor Roosevelt, *"no one can hurt you without your consent"*. Similarly, Gandhi emphasizes on the same point and says, *"They cannot take away our self-respect if we do not give it to them"*.

This may seem a bitter pill to swallow especially if you have spent a considerable part of your lifetime explaining your misery in the name of someone else's actions. However, in order to be on track pursuing your goals and purpose, you need to own up and honestly acknowledge that the choices you made yesterday are what have made you into who you are today.

Emotional or physical occurrences can cause sorrow. However, your character and your basic identity do not have to be hurt at all. As a matter of fact, the most difficult experiences that we come across become the crucibles that melt and forge our character which ultimately points us towards our purpose. Whatever does not kill us strengthens us.

Taking the Initiative

In our basic nature as human beings, we are programmed to act and not to be acted upon. We have the power to choose our response to the circumstances around us. Taking initiative has nothing to do with being aggressive, pushy or obnoxious. Instead, it has everything to do with recognizing our responsibility to make things happen around us. Many people stand and wait for something to happen or someone to take care of their affairs.

If you want to find a good job that you will enjoy for a long time, you have to be proactive and generate creative solutions to the problems that you or the organization faces. You have to seize the initiative so as to do whatever it is that is necessary in order to get the job done.

Prevail or Be Prevailed Upon

There is a huge difference between people who exercise initiative and those who do not. Life is fair in its basic sense and everyone has an opportunity to steer towards their purpose or destiny. However, if you do not utilize this opportunity to prevail, other people will prevail upon you and use you to accomplish their own purposes. Regardless of your personality, you can create a proactive culture by combining your resourcefulness and creativity. You do not have any excuse at all to be at the mercy of the environment but rather you can take the imitative and accomplish your purpose.

Listening to Your Language

Our behaviors and attitudes flow out from our paradigms. If you use your self awareness as a mirror to examine these behaviors and attitudes, you will see them in the form of underlying maps. The language we speak and the choice of our words, for instance, is an indicator of the extent to which we view ourselves as proactive people. The language of reactive people steers them away from responsibility. They usually say that they cannot do anything about the circumstances they face because it is all about fate. Proactive language looks for alternatives and it comes from a basic paradigm of determination.

The problem brought about by reactive language is that of self-fulfilled prophesy. Because you are so much reinforced in the paradigm, you become determined and produce every piece of evidence to support your belief. At some point, you feel victimized, not in charge and totally out of control of your life or destiny.

For instance, a student who wants to be excused because they have to attend a sports trip may justify his argument either to the parent or teacher by stating that failure to attend this trip can lead to him being expelled from the team. At this point, the excuse given clearly reveals a lack of control and the influence of the consequence on the choice made.

The Circle of Concern and Influence

An excellent way to becoming more aware of your degree of proactivity is to analyze where you focus your resources including time and energy. There are lots of concerns that each of us has including our children, health, work and even the vulnerability of our countries to external aggression. In an attempt to separate those things in which you have no specific emotional or mental involvement, you create a circle of concern.

As you critically examine the things within your circle of concern, it becomes clear that there are some things that you have no control over and others that you can possibly do something about them. The things which you have control over can be further regrouped into a smaller circle of influence.

By determining your allocation of energy and time between the circle of concern and the circle of influence, you can discover the extent of your proactivity. Proactive people who care about their purpose in life focus their efforts on the circle of influence. They concentrate only on the things they can do something about. The nature of their energy is magnifying, enlarging and positive which cause their circle of influence to increase.

Reactive people, on the other hand, are much engrossed in the circle of concern. They focus much about the weaknesses of others, the problems with the environment and circumstances that are totally beyond their control. The result of this focus is a disoriented and purposeless life which is hinged on blaming and accusing attitudes, increased feelings of victimization and reactive language. The negative energy which is generated by that focus added to the neglect in the areas that they could have done something, causes their circle of influence to shrink.

As long as you are working in the circle of concern and focusing your efforts on the things therein, you will not accomplish anything. Instead, your feelings of helplessness and inadequacy will increase to reinforce your dependence. On the contrary, working on your circle of influence creates positive energy that changes you and influences your subsequent actions.

The problems we face on a day-to-day basis can be categorized into three areas; direct, indirect and no control. Direct control problems involve your own behavior and can be solved by altering your habits. These are within your circle of influence. Indirect problems are caused by other people's behaviors and can be solved by changing your methods of influence such as empathy, persuasion and confrontation.

Lastly, no control problems are caused by factors that we have no control over such as situation realities and our past. Dealing with no control problems involves taking responsibility over and accepting these problems by conditioning ourselves to live with them.

Therefore, irrespective of the nature of the problem, we have no excuse to feel sad and lose the direction of our purpose. In our hands lies the first step to the solution; changing our methods of influence, changing our habits, and changing the way we see the problems we have no control over.

It is so inspiring to realize that by choosing the manner in which we respond to circumstances, we can powerfully affect our overall situation. When we change a section of the chemical formula, we affect the nature of the results. If you want to improve your situation and therefore be happy with what you do, you should concentrate on the things you have control over. There are so many ways you can use to work in your circle of influence, amongst them being a better listener, being a more dedicated and cooperative employee, or being a better student. Happiness too is a proactive choice.

5: Starting Out with the End in Mind

Oliver Wendell Holme once said *"what lies behind us and what lies before us are tiny matters compared to what lies within us."*

Imagine for a moment that you are going to a funeral and the moment you step into the chapel or funeral parlor, you notice flowers placed on top of the coffin and a soft organ music playing on the background. You also see the faces of family and friends taking turns to view the body. Such a situation definitely brings in a shared moment of sorrow and loss.

As you walk past the casket, you notice something unusual that the body inside is you; you have come face to face with yourself. All the people present have come to express their feelings of love and appreciation for your life. This may sound a little bit strange and an extension of your imagination, but assume each of the people designated to talk indeed say something about you. What do you think they will say?

None of us is an immortal being, and therefore, time will come when we shall bow out of this world. Whether you have lived your purpose or not, the point is your time will be out with no possibility of a bonus ahead. Living with the end in mind aligns your life to your purpose.

Live your life such that at the very end, at least everyone will have something positive to say about you concerning your character, contributions and achievements. Having this perspective to life will greatly enhance your personal understanding of your purpose and how to go about accomplishing it.

What It Means to Live With the End in Mind

Beginning with the end in perspective means to have a picture, an image or paradigm of the end as the point of reference by which you examine everything in life. Every part of your life including today's and tomorrow's behavior can be aptly examined in the context of your entire life and what really matters the most to you. By keeping the end in mind, you can be sure that whatever you do in any particular day does not change or violate in any way, your overall purpose. Each day in your life should contribute in a meaningful way to the vision that you have of your life.

Just like a sailor beginning his journey with the port of destination in mind, so should your life. It means that you should know where you are going so that you can understand where you are now and the steps you need to take to point you towards the right direction. The busy nature of our lives today makes it extremely easy to be caught up in activity traps trying to climb the ladder of success only to realize that the ladder is leaning on the wrong wall. It is pretty much possible to be busy without being effective.

Oftentimes, people find themselves attaining victories that are hollow. Success had come at the expense of things that they suddenly realize were far more important and valuable to them. People from every profession and walk of life including academicians, doctors, politicians, athletes, business professionals and actors often struggle to achieve a higher income, more recognition or a certain level of professional competence. What they may not realize is that this ambition to achieve their lofty goals can potentially blind them to the things that matter the most and before they realize, it may be too late.

How different can our lives be if we really know what is important for us? Having a picture of the end in mind we can manage ourselves every day so as to do the things that matter the most. You may be very busy or efficient but true effectiveness can only come when you begin with the end in mind.

Your true definition of success will be clear if you consider what you want to be said at the end of your life. Maybe the fame that you are striving for, the money, the achievement and everything else in between are not as important as your success.

It All Begins in the Mind

There are two forms of creation that define all things; mental and physical. Just like in the construction of houses, every detail of the house is first created in the mental picture before the foundation and the first nail is hammered into the structure. Unless you have a clear sense of the kind of house that you want, you cannot build one. You are made by conscious design. In your life, if you do not develop a sense of self-awareness and become responsible for your mental creations, you empower other people or circumstances outside your circle of influence to shape your life by default.

You need to stop living the scripts handed over to you by your associates, family, other people's agenda or pressures of circumstances. These scripts have their origin in people not principles, and therefore cannot lead you to your purpose.

Whether you are aware or not, the first creation (mental creation) is part of each of our lives. What you are today is the physical creation of your own proactive design or other people's agenda or circumstances.

Our inherent human capabilities of imagination, self-awareness and conscious enable us to examine our mental creations and make it possible to take charge of them and write our own scripts.

Writing Your Own Script

As mentioned above, imagination and conscience are unique human endowments that expand our proactivity level. Through imagination, you can visualize the uncreated worlds of potential and the uncharted waters that lie within you.

Conscience enables our talents to come into contact with the universal principles and the personal guidelines within which we can effectively develop them. When combined with self-awareness, imagination and conscience empower you to write your own script that will further enable you to live your purpose.

Since we already have lots of scripts handed over to us, the process of writing our scripts can be visualized more as a re-scripting process. It requires a paradigm shift that will help us to see the ineffective scripts and incorrect paradigms so that we can proactively re-script our lives.

In developing our own self-awareness, we shall discover some ineffective scripts that are deeply embedded within us, totally incongruent with our values and completely unworthy of us. You are responsible through your imagination and creativity to write new scripts that are more effective with your deepest values and principles. In an attempt to win the battle, we at times engage in things that do not win the war in the long term.

By imposing your superior size and your position of authority, you may intimidate, yell, punish or threaten a child and win. However, when you look back amidst your victory, you will be met with shuttered debris of a broken relationship with your children, an outward submission that envelops an inward rebellion and suppression of feelings that will erupt later in uglier ways.

Self-awareness, conscience and imagination can help you examine your deepest values. You can analyze the script that you live by and see whether it is in harmony with your values. Where there are inconsistencies, you can change. Make it a commitment to live out of your imagination instead of memory if you want to live out your purpose.

A Personal Mission Statement

The most effective way to integrate the end into your journey is to develop a personal mission statement also known as creed or philosophy. This mission statement focuses on what you want to be -

that is your character and what you want to do (achievements and contributions) and the values upon which your character and your achievements are to be founded.

Since we are all unique, our personal mission statements reflect our uniqueness in form, structure and content. Your personal mission statement becomes your constitution and roadmap to living your purpose.

In order to write a meaningful personal mission statement, you must begin at the center of your circle of influence. This is because this center consists of the lens through which you see the world. It is this center that enables you to deal with your values and vision. It is here that your endowment of imagination helps you to mentally create the life you were meant to live and the end that you desire. It gives you direction.

Remember, too much undisciplined leisure time has the potential to gradually waste your life. Do everything in moderation, activate your capacities, develop your talents and energize your mind and spirit. These will make your heart fulfilled and put you on the right course to achieving your purpose.

6: Leveraging on Positive Visualizations

Creative visualization is instrumental in goal achievement and task accomplishment. Numerous studies have been conducted on the area of visualization and the result has been - that when it comes to internal mental creation, our brains cannot differentiate between the real and the imagined. The imagery created in your mind has a real and tangible effect on your body. As a matter of fact, you can train your mental abilities to develop creativity, discipline and physical prowess.

Albert Einstein, one of the greatest scholars and thinkers said this about imagination. *"Imagination is more important than knowledge. For knowledge is limited to all we know and understand, while imagination embraces the entire world, and all there will ever be to know and understand."*

When you place your personal belief in the process of imagination, you can attain your goals naturally and live a purposeful life without the typical day-to-day struggles.

Building a Foundation for Visual Practice

Just like any mental or physical process, visualization requires a foundation upon which to rest. It is important that you know the strongest sensory qualities that your mind perceives. For instance, some people are affected more by words and feelings than through imagery.

If you bring to your memory, the thoughts that occupied your mental space prior to successful or failed events in the past, you will discover that your thought pattern led you to act or behave in a certain manner which attracted corresponding events and circumstances to your life. The bottom line here is that though subtle and invisible, your thoughts can create great changes through the power of visualization and imagery.

Creative Visualization

This is a mental technique which uses the power of imagination and the mind to make changes in your life and drive you towards your purpose. Through creative visualization, you can shape your character, circumstances and habits as well as attract opportunities and the things you desire in life.

The most repeated thoughts affect your subconscious mind and makes things happen. The subconscious mind controls your desires, reactions, habits and actions. These thoughts also attract corresponding circumstances. Through creative visualization, our imaginations create mental scenarios of certain events and incidences in our lives.

To a large extent, your life is the sum total of your habitual thoughts and repeated mental images. If you think positive thoughts and visualize health, success and happiness then chances are that your present circumstances will reflect these thoughts and images. It is said that *as a man thinketh so he is*. If you think failure, difficulties or problems, your life will reflect these conditions.

The more you feed your thoughts, the stronger they get and spread your tentacles around you, similar to the waves emanating from a TV or radio broadcast. A weak broadcast signal does not go far and it can hardly be perceived.

On the contrary, a strong and clear signal can be compared to concentrated thoughts which are energized by feelings and capable of creating perceivable and definite results, which in turn attract people, possessions, and objects to your life.

Imagination is the most important and powerful tool of creative visualization. Through imagination, the things you are seeing today including the cars, computers and buildings came into being.

How to Integrate Creative Visualization in Your Life

To live a life a purpose driven life where you are happy and fulfilled through the things you do, you need to bring in visualization. Virtually everyone can use visualization, and as such, there is no excuse to think that it is for a select few. Just like learning how to fly a plane or playing a musical instrument, visualization requires patience and persistence. You should put in discipline as well as time and practice until you perfect it.

The length of time it takes for you to start seeing results will depend on the vividness of your imagination and your own level of determination.

Experts suggest that you practice visualization for about 15 to 20 minutes daily, particularly at the beginning. As you master the skills and become comfortable with the technique, you can reduce the timing to a few minutes.

Research indicates that visualization works best when done in conjunction with a relaxation technique. When your body is relaxed, your mind is also relaxed and not so much under conscious control. This way, you can give it the freedom to daydream.

You can decide to take of your shoes, loosen your clothing and sit comfortably on a chair. You can also choose to take in a few deep breaths, close your eyes and picture yourself descending an imaginary steep hill or staircase.

With each step, you will feel more and more relaxed. When you are completely relaxed, you can imagine a favorite scene such as a mountain, beach or an enjoyable moment with family or friends. The kind of scene you imagine and the relative safety it gives you makes you secure and more receptive to other images.

There are a number of techniques used in visualization and imagery to summon the desired feeling and give you a direction of purpose. One of the common techniques is known as guided visualization and it involves visualization of a goal you want to achieve and then imagine yourself going through the process of achievement.

If you want to establish a business or pursue a certain career, you need to visualize yourself putting in place the financial resources, inspecting the premises and even serving your first customer.

Since thoughts combined with mental images and emotions lead to action and results, creative visualization overcomes all the sensible barriers to the attainment of your purpose. By repeating the same thoughts day in and day out, the subconscious mind is programmed to bring the visualization into reality.

Thoughts supply the purpose, aim and direction while desire supplies the energy. When combined, these components create currents of energy, both in the mental and astral worlds, which in turn create a new reality in the physical realm.

7: Mastering the Science of Personal Management

Personal management is an important process in purposeful living. It helps in directing and establishing you on the right path towards your destiny. In its simple definition, personal management refers to the planning, organizing, directing, coordinating and controlling of various aspects of your personal life so as to achieve your life purpose. In order to effectively manage yourself, you need a strong and independent will. It is the forth human endowment after imagination, self-awareness and conscience.

Why You Need Personal Management

In the complex world that we live in today, personal management is absolutely necessary as a skill if we are to recognize our hidden potentials. So as to maximize the usage of our skills and come up with solutions to our day-to-day challenges, we need a mastery of effective personal management principles.

In the pursuit of your purpose and passion, personal management helps you to control your life and build meaningful interpersonal relationships. Through personal management, you can break forth from your confines and live a fulfilled life by facing all challenges courageously. You will be able to successfully balance and coordinate your inner world including its longings, desires and imaginations with the outer world together with its relationships.

Personal management is therefore a necessity in purposeful living because it enhances success, construction of goals, construction of self and recognition of your unique abilities and inherent traits.

The Four Rules of Self Management

For you to become an effective person who knows how to manage his affairs and take control of his life, you need to observe a few rules. These rules will act as your personal guiding system as you sail towards your purpose.

The first rule is to map your life. This step will enable you to understand yourself in terms of who you are, where you are coming from and your destination. This will give you an orientation of purpose and direction. Research points out that mapping your life is the core to every success that you will ever achieve as a person.

The second step or rule is a review of your assumptions. Each one of us has a belief system and unique perspectives that we use to assess ourselves. Some of the assumptions you have as a person can potentially hinder you from attaining your life goals and becoming happy. Assumptions review allows you to peep inside yourself and count your weaknesses and strengths.

After reviewing the assumptions, you need to organize yourself and your potential to attain your desired goals in life. This is the third rule. Without self organization, even the skills you have can be easily dissolved and rendered useless.

Closely linked with self organization is the fourth rule which is development of your abilities. It includes the development and improvement of imagination, willpower and introspection among other abilities. These will enhance your capacity to express yourself.

The Power of a Strong and Independent Will

Will refers to the ability to make choices and decisions and act in accordance with them. It is a proactive approach to carrying out the program you have developed. The degree of will development in our lives is measured by the extent of our personal integrity. The higher the level of your integrity, the more independent your will is. Integrity is simply your ability to make commitments and follow them through to their very end. It is walking your talk.

Effective personal management requires that you prioritize things in life. As a self-manager, your discipline to organize the various aspects of your life should come from within. You are a disciple of your own value system. An independent will therefore give you the power to do something even when you do not want to do it as long as it is in line with your underlying values.

To develop your will, you must start by setting up and achieving small resolutions. This will give you the momentum and the zeal to move on and take larger assignments. You can boost your willpower through clarity of purpose, priority of purpose, good planning and determination.

Time Management

Time management is an essential personal management skill that helps you to organize and execute your tasks based on priorities. Each of us has the same number of hours and how we use them will determine the extent of our success or failure. The time management matrix is the commonly used tool to organize your tasks around the time available. This 4 quadrant matrix consist of activities that are classified as either urgent or not urgent and important or not important.

The first quadrant contains activities that are urgent and important. They are often called crises or problems. When you focus on this quadrant, it yields the most value adding results.

Quadrant two has activities that are important but not very urgent. They need a proper time management discipline so that you execute them on the basis of their importance.

Quadrant three has tasks that are urgent but not important. Most people misclassify these tasks in quadrant one thereby adding to the crises there. They are not as value adding as in quadrant two.

Finally, quadrant four has activities that are not urgent and also not important. They should lie at the bottom of your priority list.

In order to manage the time at your disposal, you need to prioritize and discipline yourself. Whenever the tasks overwhelm you, you should effectively delegate to reliable and capable individuals. This will give you more time to focus your energies on the remaining tasks.

8: Overcoming Negativity and Fostering Resilience

Resilience is the ability to move through difficulties and still maintain hope, wellness of mind, and positive coping methods. Resilient people are able to maintain their focus and emerge stronger after going through difficult situations.

As you move towards your purpose, you will realize that challenges will emerge that require self-confidence and new coping skills to get through. Resilience can help you to overcome any negative element that seeks to drag you off your course.

Individuals who are resilient usually display certain personality characteristics that influence the manner in which they view problems and how they solve them. Some of the personality qualities that affect resilience include:

Optimism

This is the belief that things will get better and the current challenges will be solved.

Independence

This refers to the ability to make decisions and order your own actions without having to depend on other people.

Responsibility and Control

This is the calmness and inner peace that comes by believing that you can do something to change an unfortunate circumstance.

In order to overcome negativity, you have to train yourself to think positively even when going through stressful conditions. You have the ability to change your negative thoughts into more positive ones and finding humor even when things go wrong.

The past may have been bad and the present situation is not that great, but this does not jeopardize your opportunities for the future, unless you allow the situation to do so. Your purpose in life may not be on a straight path that is lined with roses, and that is why you have to wish away the bad times and set your eyes on the final goal.

How to Develop Personal Resilience

In order to overcome challenges, you have to take deliberate steps into enhancing your resilience levels. Here are few ways you can do this:

Make Positive Affirmations

Words are powerful. Whatever you speak has the potential to become a reality. Speak positively into your life and you will be amazed at how it turns around for the better. Do not make negative confessions of weakness rather tell yourself repeatedly how strong and resilient you are.

Stir Your Determination to Achieve

Life does not always give us easy options out. We have to strive and make it a purpose irrespective of the surrounding circumstances. By increasing your determination to go against all odds, you are building your resilience reservoirs. Failure should not deter you from picking yourself up and moving on.

Strengthen your Social and Communication Skills

A problem shared is a problem half solved. By learning how to establish social bridges and enhancing our communication skills, we will be able to express ourselves and get help when faced with difficult situations on our road to success.

To overcome some challenges, all you need is a shoulder to lean on and someone to listen to you. Communication skills will also help you to seek advice when faced with a crisis concerning your purpose.

Develop your Problem Solving and Decision Making Skills

Decision making is an integral process in our daily lives. When faced with challenges and problems, our ability to conduct ourselves with an open mind can help us to sail through irrespective of the difficulty level of the problem. Since we make thousands of decisions every day, these skills will help us to maneuver and maintain focus of our ultimate goals and purpose in life.

The Brain and Resilience

Modern science helps us to learn about the biological processes of the brain and how this affects our reasoning, determination and ability to pull through challenging situations. Some parts of the brain produce chemicals that boost our happiness levels while others bring about fear and anxiety.

So to be mentally, physically and behaviorally healthy even in stressful situations, we need to change our perspectives and thought patterns. The brain responds much like programmable equipment. By speaking into the subconscious, you can awaken your potential to stand firm and display resilience even in trying times. By thinking positively on what we are currently doing, we shall find satisfaction, happiness and a reason to go on.

Environmental Influences

Much of the negativity that we encounter in life with respect to our purpose, goals, and destiny, comes from our immediate environment. For instance, if you come from a locality where a certain profession or course of life is highly discouraged or seen as being impossible, you are likely to carry with you that belief and influence, however negative it may be. Environmental influences also lower our coping mechanisms making us feel vulnerable in the face of challenges. The beauty is that you can make your own choices in life and defy the odds to emerge victorious.

Family Influence

Parents and the immediate family members have an immense role as far as shaping the purpose and destiny of their children. Many of us were brought up with certain perspectives picked from our family backgrounds. While some of these attitudes are good, some of them affect negatively making it difficult to enjoy what we do. If you were brought up in a pessimistic environment, chances are that you will not develop enthusiasm and positivity in life unless you undergo a total change of your behavioral and value system.

Therefore, to overcome negativity and enhance resilience towards your purpose, you need to develop a high sense of self-esteem. This way, you will perceive yourself as being capable, worthwhile and lovable. Even when you go through rejection and failure, your self-esteem will act as a shield to enable you bounce back and steer forward towards your destiny.

9: Leveraging on Coaching and Mentorship for Personal Development

Coaching and mentorship are capacity building tools that are very common in the area of leadership development. They have been used all over the world in different capacities depending on the existing need. Similarly in personal development, mentorship and coaching have a tremendous impact on developing personal capacities and increasing our potentials.

While coaching is more skill-focused, task oriented, directed and time -bound, mentoring concentrates more on open-ended personal development.

The Coaching and Mentoring Continuum

Instead of viewing mentorship and coaching as two distinct approaches, you can choose to look at them as different styles along the same continuum. Whether you will go for mentorship or coaching depends on your circumstances. Through mentorship and coaching, you can develop your skills, improve your performance, maximize your potential and actively become the person you desire to be.

Mentorship will take you through a psychological process that involves an exchange of practical help and guidance from the mentor to you as the mentee. This develops your personality and aligns you with your purpose.

Coaching and Mentorship Models

There are various models available that you can choose as you leverage on mentorship and coaching. Each of these models emphasizes particular attributes depending on the mentee's need.

The GROW Model

This is one of the popular models of personal development mentorship and coaching. It is a powerful framework where the coach asks you a series of questions regarding your Goal, your Reality, your Options as well as your Will.

Your Goal should be as specific as possible as well as measurable. The coach seeks to address the following questions:

- How will you know that you have achieved your goal?

- What are the expectations of other people?

- Who else needs to know about your plan and how will you inform them?

Under Reality, the coach will carefully analyze the situation you are experiencing and question you on the following strategic areas:

- What has been hindering you from achieving your goals?

- Is there anyone you know who has achieved this goal?

- What can you learn from them?

The Options section builds on the fact that you know where you are and where you want to go and so the coach will help you to address the following questions:

- What can you do as the first step to making progress?

- What else can you do?

- What will happen if you do nothing?

The **Will** stage seeks to bring out commitment to actions. Motivation is necessary in order to change and improve your performance. The questions that will guide the coach here include:

- Where does this goal fit in with respect to your personal priorities?

- What obstacles are you likely to face and how will you overcome them?

- How committed are you to achieving this goal?

- What steps must you take to achieve it?

The STEER Model

This is another coaching model that is commonly used. It stands for Spot, Tailor, Explain, Encourage and Review. It is task oriented and it is derived from the world of sport. As a solution focused model, STEER looks at what needs to be done so as to get you to the next level. It does not analyze the problem as much as it does the solution.

People-Centered Approaches

In addition to the solution focused approaches, there are people-centered approaches that take a holistic approach on your personal development. These approaches assert that people's behaviors are not just linked to their intellectual and physical abilities but to their beliefs and emotions as well. In order to change your behavior and enhance your performance towards your goals, mentors and coaches engage your emotions, values and even spiritual beliefs. Under this approach, holistic models including transformational coaching have been developed.

Key Principles of Quality Mentoring and Coaching

Coaching and mentoring takes place on a daily basis, mainly through informal processes. The problem with this kind of coaching is that it is not scheduled and structured which means that the purpose and the roles are somewhat ambiguous. For coaching and mentoring to have an impact, it should involve focused discussions which are steered by specific and agreed upon goals. The following are some top ingredients of a good and quality mentoring process.

A Learning Agreement

The learning agreement is important in order to clarify expectations and objectives to be attained through the mentorship process.

Purposeful Conversations

Structured, meaningful and constructive conversations will enable you to open up to your mentor and discuss your personal practices and beliefs. This will give the coach an opportunity to make necessary changes and amendments for your own benefit.

Empowering and Holistic

A good mentorship process is to take into account the emotional, intellectual and relational dimensions. The coach will build on your capabilities and strength to enhance your development.

Trust

A trusting relationship is necessary for mentorship to have an impact. Mentors create a safe environment where you feel free to engage even in confidential issues.

Flexibility in Approach

Depending on your unique situation, coaching should be able to adapt and address your challenges.

Impact of Coaching and Mentoring

The benefits that mentoring and coaching yield are mostly long term and purpose oriented. As an individual, mentoring will make you more confident and enhance your self-belief. It also inspires and motivates you to engage in your activities with zeal and passion. In certain circumstances, mentoring leads to self-awareness and makes you understand the contribution that you make to the society or organization. In addition, mentorship develops thinking, problem solving and people skills that are important in helping you execute your day-to-day tasks.

Mentoring and coaching therefore can help you in improving work performance, change your attitude towards life and find happiness in everything you do.

10: Living a Balanced Life

There are four dimensions that describe a healthy and balanced life. These are the spiritual, mental, social and physical. By exercising all these dimensions regularly and consistently, you will improve your life and your general outlook towards work and your purpose. This however, requires proactivity and time.

The single most powerful investment that you can ever make in your life is an investment in yourself. You are the instrument of your own performance and for you to be effective, you ought to recognize the importance of taking time to sharpen and exercise yourself.

The Physical Dimension

This involves caring for your physical body by eating right, exercising, relaxing and getting sufficient rest. Exercise is a very important activity that falls in quadrant 2 of the time management matrix. Since it is not urgent, most people wish it away and relegate it to a lower slot on their priority profile. Many of us think that we do not have sufficient time to exercise which in itself is a distorted paradigm. A minimum of 30 minutes a day is not much if you consider the benefits that such a process brings into your life. The essence of regular exercise is to enhance and improve our capacity to work, adapt and enjoy.

Spiritual Dimension

We are spiritual beings with an inclination towards a higher being. The spiritual dimension forms the core and the center of your commitment to your value system. It is a private and very important area of your life. It draws upon the resources that uplift and inspire you towards your purpose.

Mediation is one of the key exercises of the spiritual dimension. It renews, strengthens, centers and reaffirms your commitment to serve. These are the same ingredients that you need to live your purpose. Nature has a way to bequeath its own unique blessings to those who immerse themselves in it.

The Mental Dimension

Discipline study and mental development comes from formal education. However, the moment you leave this external discipline of school, many of us tend to let our minds sink into atrophy. We no longer engage in serious reading and the passion to explore new subjects dies away. We do not think analytically anymore and we do not write as creatively as we used to. Instead, we spend most of our time watching TV and engaging in extended leisure activities.

Continuing education is important because it hones and expands our minds. This is necessary for mental renewal. As a proactive and purposeful individual, you can find many ways to educate yourself and train your mind. Reading good literature gives you access into the best minds of authors and philosophers. You can set a goal reading one book a month, thereafter a book every two weeks and finally a book a week.

Remember, a person who does not read is no better off than the person who can't read.

The Social Dimension

The social dimension has its focus on interpersonal relationships, creative cooperation and empathic communication. Since our emotional and social lives are manifested through our relationship with others, they are often tied together. Renewing our social dimensions does not take as much time as the others and we can do it on a daily basis through interactions with people.

True joy in life comes from being used for a purpose that you are totally aware of. Aim to be completely used up by the time you come to the end of your time!

Conclusion

In your quest to live a purposeful life, you should zero in on the fundamental components that motivate you so that you do not spend your entire lifetime aimlessly on something that is not in sync with your potential. It is disastrous to waste your time chasing after the wrong goals, whether in life, career or business. Instead, you need to find some quality time and ask yourself some soul-searching questions.

Find out whether you are currently happy in your life. What can you do to improve it? Take care of unfinished business and find things you are passionate about. Reflect on your life as often as possible and recalibrate things when necessary. It is not a must for you to attain adulthood in order to discover your life's purpose. Always take time to think about your existential choices whenever you can. It could be at home, when commuting to work, while camping or any other occasion.

Ensure that you get your dedication right. A wrong cause or inappropriate focus can seriously cost your life or even hurt you. Make the right decisions whenever you think about your life options and always know where to focus your energies. The power of negativity is real and as significant as that of positivity. Steer clear of anything negative and destroy ideas that are inclined towards negativity. Instead, be persistent and value based in your approach to life. Sometimes the light that you need to shine on your path is right within you. It is known as the instinct.

Remember the words of Edgar Allan Poe, *"If you run out of ideas, follow the road; you will get there."*

have to work with ideas generated by your mind so as to have a clear image of what you want to construct.

The moment the image is crystallized, you can then transfer it to a construction plan. Remember that all this is done without touching anything on the ground. If you do not get the image and the blueprint clear prior to the physical construction, you may be forced to do some expensive and structurally weakening adjustments midstream. The carpenters' rule of thumb is to measure twice and cut once. The measurement part ascertains that the decision to cut is well thought out and accurate.

Once the construction starts, the usefulness of the blueprint is actualized and you keep on referring to it until the end of the process. This is what beginning with the end in mind means. The same applies to parenting and starting up businesses. This principle penetrates toe very sphere of your being.

Design or Default

In as much as things are created from the mental, then proceeding to the physical, not all creations

Made in the USA
Middletown, DE
30 March 2017